BRUMBACK LIBRARY

W9-AHG-018

3 3045 00112 3302

$13.35
j004.023 Lund, Bill,
LUN   A career in--
           computers

5/99

CHILDREN'S DEPARTMENT
THE BRUMBACK LIBRARY
OF VAN WERT COUNTY
VAN WERT, OHIO

GAYLORD

A Career in...

Computers

by Bill Lund

Capstone Press

M I N N E A P O L I S

Copyright © 1996 Capstone Press. All rights reserved. No part of this book may be reproduced in any form without written permission from the publisher.

Printed in the United States of America.

Capstone Press • 2440 Fernbrook Lane • Minneapolis, MN 55447

Editorial Director   John Coughlan
Managing Editor   Tom Streissguth
Production Editor   James Stapleton
Book Design   Tim Halldin

Library of Congress Cataloging-in-Publication Data

Lund, Bill, 1954-
   A career in-- computers / Bill Lund.
      p. cm. -- (A career in--)
   Includes bibliographical references and index.
   Summary: A guide to programming, drafting, data-entry, and other computer-related careers.
      ISBN 1-56065-290-X
      1. Computers--Vocational guidance--Juvenile literature.
   [1. Computers--Vocational guidance. 2. Vocational guidance.]
   I. Title. II. Series.
   QA76.25.L86 1996
   004'.023--dc20   95-11249
                                                         CIP
                                                         AC

13.35

Table of Contents

Chapter 1

Working With Computers

It's almost impossible to live in the United States or Canada today without operating a computer. When you play a video game, you're running a computer. Your school probably has computers in some of its classrooms. Your library may have them, too.

Computers are everywhere, and nearly every business uses them every day. Every time you use the telephone, you use a computer. What if

Computer careers can be fascinating and challenging, even for experienced workers.

Computers, and not card catalogs, now provide information in many libraries.

you buy something at a store? If they scan a
bar code to get the price, they use a computer.
Manufacturers have put computers into cars,
stereo equipment, and some household
appliances. Computers are at work when you
take an airplane trip or watch cable TV.

What's a Computer?

Basically, a computer is any machine that solves **mathematical** problems. The first computing machine was the **abacus**. It was developed in Asia more than 1,000 years ago. The abacus was a frame with beads strung on wires. It helped people do mathematical problems.

The first computer in North America was built in 1939. Now computers are everywhere, and there are many different computer careers. If you know how to work with a computer, there will be jobs open to you.

A computer operator keeps track of a complicated information system.

Managers check the work of employees and make sure the computers are working smoothly.

Operating a Computer

At first, computers might seem complicated. But computers are easier to operate today than they ever were before. In fact, you might have operated a computer today without even knowing it. Have you used an **automatic teller machine (ATM)?** Have you heated up leftovers in a microwave? Have you set up a VCR timer

Some computer technicians must know electronics to do their jobs properly.

to record a show later in the day? Then you've operated a computer.

What About a Career in Computers?

You can start a computer career right out of high school. Many employers will train you to operate their computers on the job. After you've worked as a computer operator for awhile, there will be chances to move up to a better-paying job.

If you want to design computer **software** (the **programs** that run computers) or hardware (the computing machines themselves), you will need training and experience in operating a computer.

If you're interested in working with computers, it's a good idea to take courses in computer operation or programming. Mathematics courses can also be useful. Because most computers have a **keyboard**, knowing how to type will help you get started.

Some computer jobs call for testing and repairing electronic systems.

Chapter 2
Jobs in Computers

Computer Programmer

Computers are just machines made of plastic and metal. It takes a computer programmer to make them into useful tools.

A computer programmer writes and tests computer programs (or software). A computer program is a list of steps that the computer must take in order to complete a task. For example, there are computer programs that allow you to make drawings on a computer

Programmers must learn an up-to-date programming language.

monitor. Some programs help pilots fly airplanes. Others help students to find library books. Programmers also write the steps that computers need to run video games.

Programmers write the steps in a **programming language**. This is a code that the computer can read and use. Two of the best-known programs are COBOL and FORTRAN. Most programs used in business

Many programmers must work at several monitors (computer screens) at once.

A programmer has to test his work carefully before anyone can use it.

are written in COBOL. Most programs used in science and medicine are written in FORTRAN.

It takes a programmer anywhere from a few hours to a year to write a program. The time it takes depends on how complicated the program is. When the program is completed, the programmer runs it on the computer to test it.

Any errors in the program are called **bugs**. The programmer corrects (or debugs) the program and tests it again. He or she must correct all the bugs in the program before it is ready to use.

The amount of training you need for a programming job depends on the type of work you will be doing. For some work, all you need is a high-school diploma and some computer

experience. Some programmers go to vocational school for two years to learn their trade. Programmers working on very complicated programs may go to school for four years or more.

Drafter

Whether it's the Empire State Building or a garage, every building needs a plan. **Architects** make these plans. Someone else must take the plan and put it on paper. That's the job of the drafter.

A drafter makes drawings that are used by others to build houses, office buildings, roads, machinery, spacecraft, bridges, and almost anything that can be manufactured. In their drawings, drafters show the building or object from every side. The drawings must include all the measurements and details that the builders need to know.

In the past, drafters drew plans by hand. Now most drafting is done on computers. Drafters use **computer-aided design** (CAD)

programs to create the drawing on a computer monitor. From the computer, they send the drawings to machines that can print out the plans on large sheets of paper.

Most drafters make one particular type of drawing. **Architectural** drafters draw building plans. **Aeronautical** drafters make drawings of aircraft and missiles. Electrical drafters make drawings of the complicated electrical circuits in machines, buildings, or computers.

If you enjoy drawing, you might be a good drafter. It is important for drafters to pay close attention to figures and details. One small mistake in an architectural drawing could be very expensive. Before they start work, most drafters finish high school, then go to a technical or community college for two years.

Computer Operator

Many of the computers you see in homes and business offices are **personal computers**

Drafters use special programs to create detailed plans on the screen.

Operators handle the equipment and programs for a particular business or user.

(PCs). Most large organizations, like hospitals, banks, or universities, must have much larger computers. Some use a huge computer called a **mainframe**. They hook up smaller devices, like PCs and printers, to the mainframe.

These computer **networks** can be very large and complicated. Someone must watch over them to make sure nothing goes wrong. This is the job of the computer operator.

Computer operators set the controls on computers to run programs that do particular jobs. The operators watch the equipment while the program is running. If something goes wrong, a warning message will usually appear on a computer screen. The operator must figure out what the message means. Then the operator does whatever it takes to get the computer running correctly again.

Computer operators may take care of many different kinds of equipment. They may have to watch over the printers that make copies of the information on the computer. They also might have responsibility for the **disk drives**, where the computer stores information.

Experience is very important if you want a job as a computer operator. If you have spent lots of time around computers, it will be easier to get a job as a computer operator. You can take courses in a vocational school to help you prepare. If you are hired as a computer operator, your new employer may train you.

Word Processors

The typewriter was invented in 1874. It changed the world of business forever. Letters and documents didn't have to be copied by hand anymore. They looked better and could be produced much faster.

Another revolution happened when **word processing** was developed. Word processing is a way of typing on a computer. Instead of being printed on sheets of paper, the words you type on a keyboard appear on a computer screen. You can easily change words, move sentences, or take out information that you don't need. You can even run special programs that check spelling or grammar. People who operate these programs are word processors.

Almost every organization employs word processors. That includes businesses, hospitals, government offices, and schools. Word

Almost every business office has at least one computer.

processors create letters, reports, messages, and other documents. Some word processors may take **transcription**. This means they listen to someone's voice on a tape and then type the words onto a computer screen.

Word processors often work with unusual and interesting material. They may type scientific or technical documents, or help create important letters. Almost every piece of

paper that comes out of an office is handled by a word processor.

Most word processors can begin right after high school. It is important to type quickly and to know one or two word-processing programs. Word processors must be very accurate. If you want to enter this field, take English classes to improve your spelling, punctuation, and grammar.

Data-Entry Keyer

Many people think computers are very smart. In fact, they can't work without **data**–names, numbers, and dates that the computer uses to come up with answers. Data-entry keyers supply much of this important information.

Data-entry keyers usually work on a PC that includes a keyboard, a monitor, and a printer. They use the keyboard to enter facts and figures into the computer. Other people who work with the computer can then use this information.

Data-entry keyers can work in businesses, government agencies, schools, or hospitals. The data they use may come from forms filled out by students, patients, or customers. Or they may enter facts from reports or newspapers.

Sometimes data-entry keyers enter data on a regular typing keyboard. At other times, they enter only numbers, using a **ten-key pad**. This is a group of keys that has only the numbers zero through nine.

Data-entry keyers can learn their skills on the job, right out of high school. To be a data-entry keyer, it is important to be accurate and responsible. You must also be able to carefully follow instructions and type quickly.

Medical-Record Technician

Every time a doctor or nurse checks a patient, someone must record the results. This information may include temperatures, lab results, or X-rays.

In the past, these records were written out on paper and kept in file cabinets. Now

A technician enters test results in a medical office.

computers hold nearly all medical records. The records can be stored on computer disks that take up much less space than a filing cabinet. Using disks to find old information is also much faster than checking paper files.

Medical-record technicians handle medical records on a computer. They check each medical chart to make sure that it has all the necessary information. If things are unclear or incomplete, they check with the doctor for more information. Then they enter this information into the computer.

Although computers are now common in doctors' offices, paper files are still used as well.

Medical-record technicians keep track of different trends taking place at the hospital. They might keep records on how often the hospital is treating certain types of diseases like cancer. They also keep records of the cost of each patient's treatment. They provide a record of the treatment to an insurance company, which will then help the patient pay the doctor or the hospital.

It's important for a medical-record technician to be accurate and to pay attention to details. He or she should enjoy working with figures and operating a computer. Most employers require medical-record technicians to have a two-year degree from a vocational or technical college.

Tool Programmer

Every machine is made up of parts. These must be made accurately, or they won't work with the rest of the machine. In the past, workers made many of these parts on drills or on **lathes**.

Minicomputers now run drills and lathes. With a minicomputer, this equipment can make parts more accurately and much faster. But for the minicomputer to work, a tool programmer must write and test the necessary computer programs.

To be a tool programmer, you might first work with **machinists**. These are people who make parts that fit into machines. A machinist might work with metal or plastic parts.

The machinist helps the tool programmer understand how machine parts are made. A **blueprint** shows what a part should look like, how large it is, and how it works with other parts.

Tool programmers must learn the right computer language for the minicomputer they are working with. They use that language to write the program, which then tells the computer how to make the part.

Most tool programmers need only a high-school education. They are trained on the job as machinists and programmers. There are some vocational and technical college courses in tool programming. If you are interested in a career in tool programming, it is a good idea to take high-school courses in math, physics, metalworking, computers, and drafting.

Computer equipment and telephones link this computer worker to the outside world.

Library Technician

You might think of a library as just shelf after shelf of books. But many libraries also have large and complicated computers. The people who help operate those computers are library technicians.

Computers are used in libraries to **catalog** books. The library catalog tells you where in the library you can find the book. It might also tell you if the book is available in another city or in another state. Library technicians put all this information into the computer.

Library technicians use computers to help people check books out of the library. In a library with a computer system, books have bar codes on them. These codes are made up of short black stripes and a series of numbers. The stripes tell the computer which book you have. The library technician uses a **bar-code reader** to enter this information into the computer.

In some offices, nobody uses pencil or paper. By using a computer, the workers can get much more work completed in less time.

A library card also has a bar code that identifies the person who is checking out the book. The library technician uses the bar code reader to enter the name of the person into the computer. The computer knows if the person has other books on loan, if the books are overdue, or if the person owes any fines.

Library technicians might work in public libraries or schools. They might also work in special libraries in law firms, hospitals, or government agencies. There can also be work for library technicians in businesses or museums.

Some library technicians start work right out of high school. They get on-the-job training at a library. Vocational schools offer two-year courses to help you become a library technician. Volunteering to help at your school library could give you good experience. This could help you get your first job as a library technician.

A computer operator tests equipment.

Chapter 3

Getting Ready

Here are some of the ways to prepare for a future career in computers.

Internships. Volunteer for work at a school or company where you can learn computer skills. Many businesses offer summer internship programs.

Computer Clubs. Members meet to share ideas and information. They trade tips on certain programs and applications, and may know a company that is hiring.

Read. Study books that describe the latest programs that are being used in the workplace. Study the newspaper to learn which local companies are growing. These businesses may need new workers.

Keep a Notebook. Write down useful phone numbers and addresses of local companies.

Study. Try to learn new programs on your computer, or on a computer at school if you don't have one at home.

Talk. Ask questions of your friends, family, or anyone who may know about the field. Meet with a job counselor at your school, and talk to any teachers who offer classes in computer operating.

A programmer may work on a regular computer as well as a laptop–a smaller, lighter computer that can fit into a briefcase.

Glossary

abacus–a frame with beads strung on wires. It is used for solving mathematical problems.

aeronautical–something that has to do with flight

architect–a person who designs buildings

architectural–something that has to do with the design and construction of buildings

automatic teller machine (ATM)–a bank computer that lets customers deposit and withdraw money electronically, without the help of a human teller

bar code–a series of stripes and numbers that provide information to a computer

bar-code reader–a machine that is used to enter bar codes into a computer

blueprint–a drawing that shows the plans for building something. It is usually printed on blue paper.

bugs–errors in a computer program

catalog–the list of all the books in a library

computer-aided design (CAD)–a computer program that drafters use to draw plans

data–information on a computer

disk–a computer part used to read and record information

disk drive–the device that runs a computer disk

hardware–the machines used as part of a computer system. These could be keyboards, processors, monitors, or printers.

keyboard–the set of keys you use to type on a computer

lathe–a machine that quickly spins metal, allowing a worker to shape the metal into a useful part

machinist–a person who makes machine parts

mainframe–a very large computer. Often other smaller computers are connected to it in a network.

mathematical–anything having to do with mathematics, such as addition, subtraction, or multiplication

minicomputer–a very small computer

network–a group of computers connected so that they can all work together

personal computer (PC)–a computer designed to be used by one person at a time. It usually includes a keyboard, a monitor, and a processor

program–the list of instructions that tell a computer how to complete a task

programming language–a code that a computer can read. Programs are written in programming language.

software–the computer programs that run the computer

ten-key pad–a group of ten keys that includes the digits zero through nine. It is used to enter data into a computer.

transcription–listening to someone's voice and typing the words directly into a word processor

word processing–a computer program that allows you to type and print documents

To Learn More

Burnett, Rebecca. *Careers for Number Crunchers and Other Quantitative Types.* Lincolnwood, Illinois: VGM Career Horizons, 1992.

Gordon, Susan and **Hohenadel, Kristin.** *Careers Without College: Computers.* Princeton, New Jersey: Peterson's Guides, Inc., 1992.

Primm, E. Russell, Editor-in-Chief. *Career Discovery Encyclopedia.* Chicago: Ferguson Publishing Company, 1990.

Snelling, Robert O. *Jobs!* New York: Simon and Schuster, 1989.

Some Useful Addresses

Electronics Technicians Association
604 N. Jackson
Greencastle, IN 46135

American Software Association
c/o ITAA
1616 Fort Meyer, Suite 1300
Arlington, VA 22209-9998

Computer Science Association
243 College Street
5th Floor
Toronto, Ontario M5Y 2Y1

Index

machinists, 30
mainframes, 20
medical-record technician,
26-29
microwaves, 9
minicomputers, 30
monitors, 25

networks, 20

personal computers (PCs),
19-20, 25
printers, 20-21, 25
programming, 10
programming languages,
14
schools, 5, 10, 23, 34, 37
software, 10, 13

stereo equipment, 6

ten-key pads, 26
tool programmer, 29-33
training, 10, 16
transcription, 24
typewriters, 23

universities, 20

VCRs, 9
video games, 5, 14
vocational schools, 17, 21,
29, 31, 34

word processor, 23-25